# BACKSLIDING
## ▬ Its Causes & Cure ▬

**AMBASSADOR**

Backsliding - Its Causes & Cure
© Copyright 1994 Derick Bingham

Cover photo: Noel Davidson

Printed and Published by
AMBASSADOR PRODUCTIONS LTD.,
Providence House,
16 Hillview Avenue,
Belfast, BT5 6JR
U.K.

ISBN 1 898787 02 6

# INTRODUCTION

Her face glowed with enthusiasm. She had recently become a Christian and her lifestyle had been transformed, her attitudes changed, her destiny re-directed. She was a perfect example of a "first-love Christian". It was infectious.

As I talked with that young Christian, a mother who had found Christ in her adult life, I thought of those who start out with great enthusiasm to live for Christ but who gradually backslide in their Christian lives. They get into a state where they are not utterly indifferent but they are not fully committed, either. Like the Laodiceans, they are neither cold nor hot; they are lukewarm, tepid. They are evangelical but not evangelistic. There is no emotion, no enthusiasm no urgency, no passion or compassion in their faith. They are "faultily faultless, icily regular, splendidly null".

How do Christians get into such a state? How do they get out of it? That is what this little booklet is about; it is a causes-and- cure booklet. May God use it to show many a backslider the way home.

*Derick Bingham*

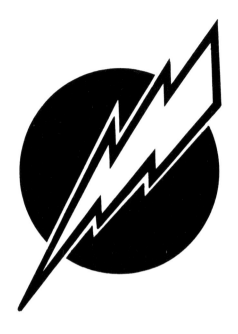

# 1. WARNING SIGNS

I well remember Space Mountain. Spending a day at Florida's Disney World had been absolutely fascinating until I noticed Space Mountain before me. I was convinced in my naivety that Space Mountain was all about the exploration of space. As I queued to enter the complex I kept coming across these signs which said, "If you are of a nervous disposition do no enter", "If you are susceptible to heart attacks do not enter", "If you have back problems do not enter", and, I thought that the signs must be for older people and carried on regardless. No experience that I can recall equals the shock I got when within minutes I rocketed into the darkness at around 70 miles per hour on one of the fastest roller coasters in the world. Believe me when I tell you that I get sick on roundabouts! I thought I was going to die! I smile a lot about it now, but it was no smiling matter at the time.

Disney World, though, is fantasy world, isn't it? Life is real. When God puts up warning signs along life's journeys it pays to heed them. We must not say, "That's for older people", or "That's for younger people". It is to our spiritual advantage to stop and say, "That's for me!". Let's check out some of the warning signs God puts up in the Scriptures. It will save a lot of backsliding and subsequent heartache if we obey them. Let me list a few.

# BEWARE OF ALCOHOL

The story of Noah does not end, unfortunately, with a very pleasant record. When the man who found grace in the eyes of the Lord settled down after the trauma of the flood, he planted a vineyard. One day he got drunk and was found by his sons lying naked in his tent. The whole sorry episode had far-reaching repercussions for him and his family.

The Bible shows that alcohol is deceitful and "he who is deceived thereby is not wise". Twenty per cent of males and ten per cent of females in the adult population are seriously involved with alcohol. Alcohol disease is said to be the third public health problem after cancer and cardiovascular disease. The mortality of dependent and problem drinkers is three to four times that of the general population, and life expectancy is reduced by about fifteen years. Each year between eight and fourteen million working days are lost through alcohol abuse. Eight hundred million pounds are lost to industry and sickness absence due to alcohol. The Brewing Industry spends four billion pounds in advertising and three hundred thousand in research into the effects of alcohol. Advertising is directed towards young people. In a sample of sixteen to twenty-four year olds on Saturday night drinking ten per cent had drunk more than seventeen units of alcohol (example, eight and a half pints of beer) and forty per cent of twenty to twenty-four year old males were regularly over the legal limit. In about eighty per cent of all serious road accidents, alcohol is implicated. In ninety per cent of suicide attempts alcohol is involved. It causes depression to worsen, leads to impaired thinking processes, and produces impetuous actions.

My friend, Dr. Adam Hanna, writing on the subject of 'The Christian and Alcohol' recently quoted a medical expert involved in the prevention of alcohol abuse. The expert said, "Primary prevention is the activity that stops the non-hazardous drinker becoming a hazardous one, and health education is directed to this end, but there seem to be powerful, if ill-defined forces pushing many across that threshold". Dr. Hanna points out that in small or large doses the effect of alcohol on the body (the brain) is always depressant, inhibitory, i.e. negative.

Paradoxically the effect of small doses appears to be to relax, to reduce sense of stress, to give feeling of pleasure or well-being, but alcohol does that by actually depressing the normal inhibitory systems in the higher centres of the brain. For example, prepandial "drinks" at a lunch or party are supposed to lower people's inhibitions and allow them to mix more freely, to give them a feeling of excitement or pleasure, and to reduce the normal stress of meeting strangers - but they do this by "cheating" and exerting a depressant action on protective natural inhibitions rather than giving an added excitatory action.

In any event this effect is short lived and often it takes more and more to produce the same effect. Along with this feeling of relaxation or pleasure, alcohol in small doses does several other things.

It produces a loss of general efficiency, reduces one's critical abilities, slows one reflexes, and allows one's more basic instincts to emerge. It is easy therefore to respect deeply the person (many of them non-Christians) who in the light of this picture remain life- long teetotallers. They have wisdom on their side, however else they may be regarded. The word of Scripture is a warning to us all; "Do not be drunk with wine, in which is dissipation; but be filled with the Spirit".

## BEWARE OF LYING

The story of Abraham gives a very clear warning. He arrived in Canaan and found himself in a famine situation, panicked, fled into Egypt and lied to Pharoah that his wife was his full sister because he was afraid they would kill him and take her. God sent a plague on Pharoah's house as a result, Abraham's lying was discovered and he was thrown out of Egypt.

It was not until he got back to the point where he had got off track at a place called Bethel and there "called on the name of the Lord" that he experienced restoration from his backsliding. Forty years later, though, he again ignored the warning sign and lied again to subsequent harrowing trouble. Later in the Scriptures we read of Jacob, though having a Godly father, backslid very seriously. He deceived his old blind father into blessing him and in turn, many years later, his own sons deceived him with a blood-stained coat into believing that his beloved child Joseph was dead. What we sow, we reap.

## BEWARE OF HASTE

Moses desperately wanted to free God's people. At forty years of age he saw an Egyptian beating a Hebrew and decided to kill him. It was a hasty action and led to forty years in a literal as well as spiritual wilderness. He should have waited for God's time. The little word "Selah" in the Psalms means "pause". Say it often.

## BEWARE OF GREED

Achan was in Joshua's army when they took the city of Jericho. The army was warned by God not to loot; the silver and gold and vessels of bronze and iron were to be given into the Lord's treasury. Achan, though, was greedy, and stole gold and silver in Jericho for himself. As a result the whole of the nation of the Children of Israel were held up in their progress into the Promised Land until Achan's sin was dealt with. The warning from Achan's life shows that one backslider can do as much and more damage to the progress of God's work and God's people than the enemies of the Lord.

## BEWARE OF IMMORALITY

Samson was a He-man with a She-weakness. Gifted with special strength from God, he fooled about with his gift instead of using it to God's glory. The most gifted believers are not always the best behaved, are they? The prostitute at Gaza, and the subtle Delilah in the valley of Sorek, made Samson court lust, but that which appeared to him as soft as down became, before it was finished, a flaming vulture. Solomon too, the wisest man in all the earth became an effeminate fool and allowed women to turn his heart away from the Lord. His father, David, the man after God's own heart, found that a moment's indulgence wrecked his family and brought about the severing of his kingdom. The blame, please note, was not left at Bathsheba's door but David's. Purity, Christian, is power.

## BEWARE OF POPULARITY

Saul, Israel's king, had Israel's army mustered at Gilgal. His enemy, the Philistines, were massed against him with thirty thousand chariots and six thousand horsemen and people "as the sand which is on the seashore in multitude". Saul had been commanded by the prophet Samuel to wait for the prophet's arrival to offer a sacrifice to the Lord before he went into battle. He waited five, six and even seven days and when Samuel did not show up, Saul's patience began to run out. His men began to scatter. You can almost hear them, can't you? "What an indecisive man is Saul". So, to be popular, he disobeyed the prophet and the Lord's commandment and offered up the sacrifice. It cost him his throne.

Peter, of course, in New Testament days, had the same problem; he wanted to be liked. His Lord and Saviour was bound and interrogated at the High's Priest's house and the servant girl there asked Peter if he were one of Christ's disciples. The result? Wanting to be liked and wanting to be popular Peter denied his Saviour on the spot. He was to regret it all his days. Beware of popularity.

Voltaire was once going past a crowd queueing to see one of his plays. "Look at that crowd, queueing to see your play", said a friend. "The same crowd would come to see me hung", he said. Too right.

## BEWARE OF HYPOCRISY

No prophet ever thundered against hypocrisy like Isaiah. The Bible's word for hypocrisy has to do with play-acting, it has to do with being two-faced in a relationship with God. It is to be one thing when before God and another thing when before people. Hypocrisy just will not "wash" with God. He hates it and if, as a Christian, you are being hypocritical, then you are without doubt in a backslidden condition. If you doubt me, just meditate on these words of God spoken by Isaian to the people of Israel. "To what purpose is the multitude of your sacrifices to me? I have had enough of burnt offerings ... when you come to appear before Me, who has required this from your hand, to trample My courts? Your New Moons and your appointed feasts My soul hates; they are a trouble to Me, I am weary of bearing them. When you spread out your hands, I will hide My eyes from you; even though you make many prayers I will not hear". (Isaiah 1; 12-15).

## BEWARE OF FALLING IN LOVE WITH THE AGE YOU LIVE IN

At the very end of the Apostle Paul's life, when he was under house-arrest, there appears a little line in a letter which he wrote to his young friend, Timothy, which is quite haunting. "Demas", he wrote, "has forsaken me, having loved this present world, and has departed for Thesslonica". (2 Timothy 4; 10). What had happened? In plain language, Paul's fellow helper Demas (Philemon 24) had left the track of service; he had become a backslider.

We may be quite sure that it was not a sudden collapse. The crisis, when it came, was certainly a matter of a single fatal decision but, just as a marriage doesn't suddenly collapse without other events occurring first, just as a building doesn't suddenly collapse without cracks or faults appearing somewhere, so before Demas's defection came, his love for Christ had been burning low.

In Demas's soul, at one time, the thought of Christ's Kingdom had thrilled him, he had longed for the coming of Christ, but now, says the Bible, "he loved this present age". What made the difference? The most probable reason was that identification with Christ was becoming a very serious matter. Nero had burst into a mad fury and the Christians were bearing the brunt of his murderous mania. Paul, his friend, was under house-arrest and the verdict might go against him. Demas probably feared arrest and the Province of Macedonia would have been an infinitely safer place to live, especially since Thesslonica was a free city under Greek local

Government. Demas preferred to win his own comfort than to win the lost. He loved this present age while Paul loved Christ's appearing. Paul looked to the future. Demas wanted more of the present. Paul finished the course; Demas left the track. Let's be warned. He who loves this present age will soon become a widower. Let's never be tempted to retain situations and desert Christ, to avoid derision, and miss the reward of confessing the Lord. May the Lord find that we choose Him rather than our own ease and prefer to face the storm by His side to basking in the sunshine alone.

In the great Cathedral in Frieberg, Germany, the organist would allow no-one to play the massive pipe organ but himself. He guarded the superb instrument, jealously. One day a man came into the Cathedral and gently asked if he could play it. The organist was extremely reluctant to give permission but eventually relented. The stranger played the organ like it had never been played before. "Can I ask your name?", asked the Cathedral organist. "Felix Mendelsson" was the reply. "To think", the Cathedral organist used to say, "I very nearly didn't let the Master play the organ".

Let's make sure the Master of our lives has His way. Let's heed the warning signs He has put out for us in His Word. If we do we will never regret it for we will be preserved from backsliding and be enabled to live our lives to His glory.

# 2. TWO BACKSLIDERS INVESTIGATED

He was a true believer. He hated wrongdoing with a holy hatred. He was a child of God and an heir of the Kingdom. It would be easy to read his case-notes and go away saying he was a no-good, but, the Bible won't let us. Yet, he became a backslider. So much so, two angels had to virtually drag him out of the city where he lived before God destroyed it. His name was Lot. How on earth did he get into such a spiritual state?

It is true that Sodom, the city where Lot lived, was a very sinful place, but, Lot did not become accustomed to what went on in it. He was a just and righteous man and, 2 Peter 2; 7-8 says he had his righteous soul tormented from day to day by seeing and hearing the lawless deeds of the unrighteous around him. Yet, despite this, Lot slipped into a tepid state of soul. What word sums it all up? The answer is given in Genesis 19; 16. It says, "He lingered". H e knew the awful condition of the city where he lived, hated its practices, but, when two angels were sent from God urging him to get out, he lingered.

He believed God always kept His Word, but, he lingered. "Arise", they cried, "Take your wife and your two daughters who are here, lest you be consumed in the punishment of the city". Yet, he lingered until the angels "took hold of his hand......and brought him out and set him outside the city".

What was it that drew Lot into such a dithering, lukewarm commitment to his Lord? The answer is that he made a wrong and selfish choice in his early life. There was strife between the herdsmen of his uncle Abraham and his own herdsmen when Lot had lived with Abraham and Abraham decided they had better split up. Abraham said, "You take left, I'll go right; you go right, then I'll go left".

What did Lot do? Without any prayer for guidance he stood up and looked out the best land and water in all the country around him and without a moment's hesitation "chose for himself all the plane of Jordan". Note those two words " for himself".

Lot well knew the name and character of the city of Sodom that lay in the rain and sunshine before him but, as J. C. Ryle commented, "Lot's cattle were already up to their stomachs in the grass around Sodom and that was heaven on earth to Lot..... The pasture was rich, the land was good. He wanted such country for his flocks and herds and before that argument all scruples and doubts, if indeed he had any, at once went down".

First he "looked" (Genesis 3; 10), then he "pitched his tent towards Sodom" (Genesis 3; 12). Then he "dwelt" in Sodom (Genesis 14; 12).

Nothing wrong with Sodom if God wants you there. Nothing wrong with "well watered plains" if God sends you there. But, better a wilderness and little money and the blessing of God and the joy of the Lord in your soul than to go to Sodom out of the will of God. Lot did no good in Sodom. Not one of his neighbours believed his witness nor cared one hoot for his opinion. His salt lost its savour; his wife turned into a pillar of salt when she disobeyed God an d his two daughters escaped to do the Devil's work. We leave Lot in the pages of Genesis, a poor drunken, miserable wretch living in a cave.

So, Christian, beware of your choices. Remember when you choose a house or a flat in which to settle down, comfort, good location and reasonable rent or price isn't everything. When you choose a career it will cost you nothing if you make a lot of money and have lean-ness in your soul at the same time. Don't linger; ask God's guidance before you make a choice and put Him first in all that you do. If you make selfish choices you will end like Lot, saved from the fire but losing out eternally on the reward. (Read very carefully Paul's warning in 1 Corinthians 3; 12-15).

Let us now investigate a character who was the very opposite to Lot. He obeyed God meticulously in his early life. He chose wisely and prayerfully. With 3OO men and the power of God he turned an army that lay like "sand by the seashore in multitude" into flight. Even before he defeated the Midianites he cut down the totem pole to a false god in his own father's back yard and instead of his father turning against him, his father became his greatest supporter. He was used by God to restore his own father from gross backsliding. His name? Gideon.

What happened to such a godly man? How did the man who was able to control the unity of his army through prayer and who was able to keep the supply line of food going when most of his fellow compatriots had fled to the hills for fear of the enemy, become a backslider? It all started with him losing his temper.

If we could leave the story of Gideon with his subduing of the Midianities, Gideon's story would have been a happy story indeed, but, the Bible record of his life goes on in all realism to tell us that the wonderful fruits of victory w ere flawed. It shows us that Satan is a very dirty fighter. We read that as Gideon pursued the Midianites, the men of Ephraim, part of God's people, couldn't rejoice in Gideon's victory. Why? Because they had not been "called up" and since they didn't have a part in his victory, they couldn't rejoice.

They even "gave off" to Gideon as he was pursuing the enemy during . his great victory. Jealousy, of course, always hinders the work of God. "Why", said Gideon, "What have I done in comparison with you? Is not the gleaning of the grapᴕ of Ephraim better than the vintage of Abiezer?". Gideon, in other words, took the low place; he subtly reminded the men of Ephraim of their position as the largest tribe in Israel who lived in a much richer track of country than he did. He knew that a soft answer always turns away wrath. So, he let them go, wasn't diverted by the Devil's ploy and went on pursuing the enemy.

If only Gideon had kept up such a wise attitude. But the Devil pursued him yet again and tried to "ditch him" with the men of Succoth. The men of Succoth had no fewer than seventy elders and seven princes at their head. The y were part of God's people and Gideon asked them, "Please give loaves of bread to the people who follow me, for they are exhausted". But the leaders of Succoth replied that since Gideon hadn't won yet, why should they give bread to his army?

Mark it well that the men of Succoth were the Lord's people and Gideon was the Lord's appointed representative. When they refused to help Gideon, they were in reality refusing to help the Lord. Yet, it is at this very point that Gadeon began to slip back. Backsliding, you see, can begin by our reaction for life is ten per cent what happens to us and ninety per cent how we react to it.

Why did Gideon not let them go, like he did the men of Ephraim? I do not know, but, instead of answering them quietly and going on with his work for the Lord, he promised that when he returned after victory over the enemy he would t ear their flesh with the thorns of the wilderness and with briars. And he did just that. Nasty, miserable thorns that the curse produced were used by Gideon to cut his brethren down to size. He found a young man from the city, interrogated him, wrote down the seventy elders names, took the thorns of the wilderness and thrashed the elders of Succoth. Later at a place called Penuel Gideon got the same treatment as he had received at Succoth and he came back and tore down the tower of Penuel and killed the men of the city.

See what backsliding can do? Whose side was Gideon fighting on, now? Would the men of Penuel not need their defence?

Would the men of Succoth not need their elders? Temper was the undoing of Gideon at the end of a time of great blessing. He was a great man but he didn't remove the needle in his tongue. Anger is a God-given emotion but bad temper is a sin. Gideon ended up fighting the Lord's people instead of the Lord's enemies. It marred his great witness.

Let's learn lessons from the lives of Lot and Gideon for if we do it will be a cure for much backsliding and a prevention of more.

❖ Beware of the choices you make (Proverbs 3; 5-6).

❖ Make sure that your choices in life are not made from a selfish motive (Genesis 13; 11).

❖ Do not "linger" between commitment to God's command and commitment to your own desires (Genesis 19; 15-16).

❖ Make sure that you do not allow your choices to lead you to material wealth at the cost of sending lean-ness into your soul (Psalm 106; 15).

❖ Make sure you do not merely escape hell and lose out on eternal rewards in Heaven by building "wood, hay and stubble" in your life (1 Corinthians 3; 12-15).

❖ Learn to ignore petty disagreements (Proverbs 19; 11).

❖ Refrain from close association with anger-prone people (Proverbs 22; 24-25).

❖ Keep a close check on your tongue (Proverbs 15; 1).

❖ Control your anger or it will control you (Proverbs 25; 28).

# 3. A LETTER TO BACKSLIDERS

How would you feel if, at your local church, you received a letter directly from the Lord? It would make an interesting Sunday morning if it was read out, publicly, detailing the Lord's view of what He thought about the spiritual condition of your local church and all its members.

Other opinions of your local church could be argued with but the Lord's opinion is different.

He has full executive power and authority over His church and, being the perfect One, His summary of how you stood would allow no arguments. This Judge's opinion is final.

Such was the situation when the Apostle John received a revelation of the Lord's Word to the seven churches recorded in the book of the Revelation. The letters were actually written to seven churches existing at the time in Asia but they carry an even wider message because they give a picture of seven conditions of Christians and their church life to be found continuously in the history of the Church of Christ.

Their message is very relevant to our subject of backsliding for they give a clear "causes-and-cure" analysis of certain spiritual conditions.

The letters contain good things Christ found in His churches but they also contain Christ's complaints and His superb counsel as to how His people could reverse their condition.

No Christian could study them but to his or her advantage. Let's have a look at a few of these letters.

## THE EPHESUS LETTER

The Church in the wealthy, cultured but corrupt city of Ephesus had been planted by Paul, greatly aided by his friends Aquilla and Priscilla, the tentmakers. Had you visited it you would have reckoned it to be the most outstanding Christian church you ever saw in your life. True church order was in place, the ministry was first rate, the administration was fine. The Lord had seven good things to say about the Ephesian church.

"I know your works", said the Lord. Here was no passive group of Christians; they were very active for their Master. "I know your tribulation". These Christians were not afraid of the cost of living for Christ.

"I know your patience". They were no quitters, these Ephesian Christians. On and on they went, week in and week out, year in and year out. "I know you cannot bear those that are evil", is Christ's opinion of the way they guarded their fellowship from impure men and women. "I know you have tested those who say they are apostles and are not and have found them to be liars", comments the Lord. No false doctrine found its way into the church at Ephesus.

"And you have persevered and have patience and have laboured for my Name's sake and have not become weary". Persecution didn't swamp the courage of the saints at Ephesus. They were true to their Lord.

What, then, could possibly be wrong with such a church? How could you find a backslider in the whole place? Truth was, they were all backsliders! "Now", says the Lord of the churches, "I have this against you that you have left your first love". That's it! A single sentence, but, devastating in its analysis. The church was busy, orthodox, sound, faithful but lacking in emotion and enthusiasm. You know how it is. A fellow falls in love and first love defies analysis. Ask him why he loves and he can't tell you. His love is pure, unselfish, ardent, humble. It isn't forced, it isn't a duty, it is full of tenderness. Dr. G. Campbell Morgan put it perfectly when he said the Lord no longer heard "the song at the unusual hour" from the Ephesian Christians . They were "faultily faultless, icily regular, splendidly null".

And the cure? "Repent therefore from where you have fallen; repent and do the first works, or else I will come to you quickly and remove your lampstand from its place - unless you repent". The Lord tells them to turn back in heart and purpose to their first attitude to Him. He tells them to believe in Him in the way they used to.

Else? Else despite all their ice-cold purity and orthodoxy, their church will be removed. The message to the backsliders of Ephesus or the backsliders of this present century could not be clearer. Selah.

## THE PERGAMOS LETTER

We would probably called Pergamos a "New Age" city in our day.

Aesculapis, the god of medicine was worshipped there and the special aspect of this worship was the study of the secret springs of life. Like all Nature worship, it was sincere but brought with it much corruption. The church at Pergamos was faithful to the Lord, even to the death, for one of its members, Antipas, was martyred for Christ, there. But they had a problem. Some of their number believed "the doctrine of Balaam" which simply stated held that since you were the Lord's you needn't worry too much about how you behaved.

Many backsliders are like that. Because they believe that once a person is saved, they are always saved (which, incidentally, I also believe), they also think that a believer's behaviour will make no difference to their Heaven.

Nothing could be further from the truth. A study of the story of the prodigal son and the immediate parable of the shrewd manager which follows it (Luke chps. 15 and 16) will show very clearly that the Christian will lose out on eternal reward by ungodly behaviour after their conversion.

Not only will people who "hold the doctrine of Balaam" lose out, eternally, their doctrine is a pernicious, dangerous poison in the body of the local church. The Lord counsels the Christians at Pergamos to deal with these people by showing both them and their doctrine no toleration. He warns them to discipline these people or else He will discipline them Himself.

There is, in the letter to Pergamos, a beautiful promise given to the person who overcomes. To such an overcomer the Lord says He will give a "white stone, and on the stone a new name written which no one knows except him who receives it". What does this mean? A white stone was given to a person who, after a trial, was justly acquitted. It was also given to one who returned victorious from battle. It was the reward of victory. The white stone was given to a person who was made a free man of the city. But, there is an even greater meaning.

There was the white stone known as the tessara hospitalis. Two men, friends, about to part, would divide a white stone in two, each carrying with him half, upon which was inscribed the name of the friend. It may be they would never meet again, but that stone in each case would be bequeathed to a son, and sometimes generations after, a man would meet another, and they would find that they possessed the complementary halves of one white stone, and their friendship would be at once created upon the basis of the friendship made long ago.

So it is that for the overcomer there is the white stone of acquittal, the white stone of victory, and the white stone of citizenship, which marks the freedom of the city of God. Best of all, though, is the white stone of unending friendship, my name written on His half, His Name written on mine.

The central message of the Pergamos letter to the backslider of today is an extremely solemn one. It is that the test of doctrine is purity of conduct and character. What we believe is extremely important but how we behave is equally so.

## THE SARDIS LETTER

The Lord's complaint about the Christians at Sardis was startling, to say the least. "I know your works", He said, "That you have a name that your are alive, but you are dead. Be watchful and strengthen the things that remain, that are ready to die, for I have not found your works perfect before God". It was a devastating appraisal of a very frightening spiritual condition. What was it? It was outward observance of spiritual things and inward spiritual deadness. Nothing they did satisfied God. It looked great on paper, it sounded wonderful in the committee room, but death reigned. The church at Sardis had a wonderful reputation amongst others but before God it was dead.

"Establish the things that remain", counsels the Lord. If the church at Sardis was dead, what on earth could have remained? The unfulfilled things. They met to break bread and drink wine in remembrance of Christ's death but now they were called on to truly do that.

They met to pray but now they were called on to truly pray. They had gifts, now they were to exercise those gifts to the full to God's glory. No church can exist on mere formal gatherings or on mere organisational ability, it needs to respond to the leadership of the Spirit of God which is its vital force. What we need here in the western world is not yet another Christian denomination but a mighty breath of God through us as we are, today.

## THE LETTER TO THE LAODICEANS

If ever there was a word from the Lord to backsliders it is found in His letter to the Laodiceans. "I know your works, that you are neither cold nor hot. I could wish that you were cold or hot. So then, because you are lukewarm, and neither cold nor hot, I will spew you out of my mouth. Because you say, 'I am rich, have become wealthy, and have need of nothing' - and do not know that you are wretched, miserable, poor, blind, and naked - I counsel you to buy from me gold refined in the fire, that you may be rich; in white garments, that you may be clothed, that the shame of your nakedness may not be revealed; and anoint your eyes with eye salve, that you may see. As many as I love, I rebuke and chasten. Therefore be zealous and repent.

Behold I stand at the door and knock. If anyone hears My voice and opens the door, I will come in to him and dine with him, and he with Me."

I want to use the teaching in this letter to bring our study to its conclusion. The letter is both exquisitely sad and, yet, exquisitely beautiful. Here is a church which is neither hot nor cold. It thought it was rich and had need of nothing and, yet, says the Lord, "You are wretched, miserable, poor, blind and naked".

Note its spiritual condition. It wasn't frozen, nor was it boiling. It was lukewarm, tepid. The Lord said to them, "I could wish you were cold or hot", but He detests their lukewarmness. As someone once put it, "They were evangelical but not evangelistic". Is there anything, in all the world, which is so repugnant to the Lord as a tepid church? The Lord so detested their lukewarmness - He said He would spew them out of His mouth.

He did not mean He was going to break His eternal relationship with them but it did mean He was about to take the church at Laodicea away from its place of witness. He was about to put out the light of its witness-bearing. He had not done it yet, but He was about to.

Could it be that you are just like the Laodiceans? He said that they were "wretched", that is, carrying a burden where outwardly they appear to be doing very well and in need of nothing. Actually their wealth was hindering them. Is that you? He said they were "miserable", that is, pitiable. He pitied them. Is that you? He said they were "poor", that is, so poor all they had was money! Is that you? He said they were "blind", that is, they could see nothing clearly! Is that you? He said they were "naked", that is, outwardly wearing gold and beautiful clothes but gold that was tarnished and clothes that were moth-eaten in the light of a robe of true service for Christ. Is that you?

What was the cure the Lord offered? "I counsel you", He said, "to buy from Me gold refined in the fire, that you may be rich". The Lord has what the Laodiceans and any other backslider lacks. He has true wealth. If any backslider will get down on their knees before the Lord and admit their spiritual condition, then the Lord will reward them with things that He considers to be wealth, things that have eternal consequences, gold that never tarnishes. He pleads that you buy that kind of gold from Him and be truly rich. Will you?

He then promises "white garments that you may be clothed". Sin can be forgiven, the backslider can be restored, and we need, as Paul put it, no longer make provision for the flesh but we need to "put on the Lord Jesus". What a covering for our spiritual nakedness!

Finally He says, "Anoint your eyes with eye salve, that you may see". No chemist's potion ever had a more powerful effect than the Lord's eye salve on a backslider's eyes. He can make you see things as you never saw them before. He can give you insight the world knows nothing of. Don't stumble on in a half-baked, lukewarm, tepid, neither hot-nor-cold Christian life. Buy the Lord's gold, put on His garments, let Him, this very moment place His eye salve on your tired and weary eyes. He says, "Behold I stand at the door and knock. If anyone hears My voice and opens the door, I will come in to him and dine with him and he with Me". These beautiful words were first spoken to a backsliding church. They are now spoken to backsliders everywhere. Will you open up the door and let Him in? The choice is yours.

# Other Pathway Booklets
# in this series include:-

❖ **WORRY** - A Biblical Answer to the King of all Addictions

❖ **SUFFERING** - A Biblical Perspective on Life's Greatest Puzzle

❖ **VALUES** - Things Worth Standing Up For

❖ **GUIDANCE** - Biblical Direction For Life's Choices

*£1.75 each plus 25p postage and packing*

Ambassador Productions Ltd
16 Hillview Avenue,
Belfast, BT5 6JR
Northern Ireland

Derick Bingham is a Bible teacher with the
Crescent Church, Belfast. The following is a selection of
message tapes from "Tuesday Night at the Crescent"

# JOY - THE CHRISTIAN'S SECRET STRENGTH

## A study of Paul's letter to the Philippians

Confidence: The basis of joy

Tough Circumstances: The test of joy

Consistency: The progress of joy

Christlikeness: The completion of joy

Self: The enemy of joy

Friends: The fellowship of joy

Pride: The killer of joy

Principle: The anchor of joy

Citizenship: The mark of joy

Harmony: The music of joy

Worry: The disturber of joy

Contentment: The fruit of joy

Power: The fuel of joy

# HOME, WHERE LIFE MAKES UP ITS MIND

Is family life facing extinction?

What is God's blueprint for marriage?

Is monogamy God's will?

Is marriage God's plan for everyone?

The most unpopular requirement for marriage

Are we undertaking marriage too lightly?

Is marriage worth waiting for?

Why do couples fight?

Don't be a passive parent

How should we discipline our children?

Living with teenagers

When the unbearable is inescapable

Tell debt do us part

Commitment is the key

# THE RELUCTANT HERO

## A study of the life of Moses

Born after midnight
Lessons learned from failure
Burning bridges or bushes
Lord here am I, send Aaron!
When they all stand up against you
Plaques that preach
The night nobody slept
Between the devil and the deep Red Sea
Is the Lord testing you?
Giving up a good thing for a better
Reverence, the forgotten attitude
The believers occupational hazards
What bad temper can do
Do shadows frighten you

# THERE IS AN ALTERNATIVE

## Studies in the Sermon on the Mount

The most radical lifestyle, ever
The richest self-fulfilment possible
How to make life tasty
Overcoming anger and lust
Divorce and oathtaking: are they permissible?
Should we turn the other cheek?
How to love your enemy
Beware! Religious performance now showing
Are you into prayer and fasting
The tragedy of Mr Facing Bothways
Are you a worrier?
Putting an end to labelling people
The narrow way doesn't get broader
The simple secret of an unsinkable life
The amazing Lord Jesus

# DOES GOD STILL GUIDE?

## Biblical principles on knowing God's will for your life

Guidance: Why do we need it?
Guidance: When does it come?
Guidance: How do we know it?
Guidance: Can we stray from it?
Guidance: Does prayer affect it?
Guidance: Why is it often delayed?
Guidance: So, what about it?

# THE ROAD LESS TRAVELLED BY

## A study of Christ's influence in life's decisions

When you are facing temptation
When you are facing misunderstanding
When you are facing doubt
When you are facing inadequacy
When you are facing pain
When you are facing disqualification
When you are facing shame
When you are facing success addiction
When you are facing a need for grace

Audio cassettes are £3:00 each
(add 25p post and packing)
Available from :-
Ambassador Productions Ltd.
16 Hillview Avenue
Belfast BT5 6JR
Northern Ireland